BACK FROM NEAR EXTINCTION

GRAY WOLF

by Tammy Gagne

Content Consultant
Ryan Scott
Regional Supervisor, Region I, Wildlife Conservation
Alaska Department of Fish and Game

Core Library

An Imprint of Abdo Publishing
abdopublishing.com

abdopublishing.com

Published by Abdo Publishing, a division of ABDO, PO Box 398166, Minneapolis, Minnesota 55439. Copyright © 2017 by Abdo Consulting Group, Inc. International copyrights reserved in all countries. No part of this book may be reproduced in any form without written permission from the publisher. Core Library™ is a trademark and logo of Abdo Publishing.

Printed in the United States of America, North Mankato, Minnesota
072016
012017

Cover Photo: Holly Kuchera/Shutterstock Images
Interior Photos: Holly Kuchera/Shutterstock Images, 1; iStockphoto, 4; Frank Pali/All Canada Photos/Glow Images, 7; Andy Gehrig/iStockphoto, 9, 14; David Parsons/iStockphoto, 11; Dennis W. Donohue/Shutterstock Images, 17, 43; Red Line Editorial, 18, 29; Tenley Thompson/iStockphoto, 20; Yellowstone's Photo Collection, 22; Garrett Cheen/The Livingston Enterprise /AP Images, 24, 27; John E. Marriott/All Canada Photos/Glow Images, 30; Steve Kazlowski/DanitaDelimont.com "Danita Delimont Photography"/Newscom, 32, 45; Clint Austin/The Duluth News-Tribune/AP Images, 35; Brendan Oates/US Fish and Wildlife Service, 37; Darrin Underwood/iStockphoto, 39

Editor: Marie Pearson
Series Designer: Jake Nordby

Publisher's Cataloging-in-Publication Data

Names: Gagne, Tammy, author.
Title: Gray wolf / by Tammy Gagne.
Description: Minneapolis, MN : Abdo Publishing, 2017. | Series: Back from near
    extinction | Includes bibliographical references and index.
Identifiers: LCCN 2016945429 | ISBN 9781680784671 (lib. bdg.) |
    ISBN 9781680798524 (ebook)
Subjects: LCSH: Gray wolf --Juvenile literature.
Classification: DDC 599.773--dc23
LC record available at http://lccn.loc.gov/2016945429

CONTENTS

CHAPTER ONE

OUT OF DANGER?

The gray wolves have been trailing the caribou herd for days. Together they patiently stalk their prey. The wolves remain close yet silent. The caribou's hoofbeats echo across the open plain. Making a move then would be too risky. Sunlight had melted much of the snow on the ground. The caribou could easily outrun the predators here. Instead, the wolves wait for the right moment.

The forest's shade keeps snow from melting as fast as it does on the plain.

The wolves gain the advantage in the woods. The snow is not melted there. The wolves' wide, round paws help them dash across the snow's crust. The caribou's heavier bodies cause their hooves to sink to the ground. The slowest caribou begins to fall behind the rest of the herd.

Moments after the prey crosses into the forest, the caribou in the back catches sight of the predators. It scrambles to move to the middle of the herd. But trying to move quickly through the snow only slows the animal down. The wolves surround the caribou as its herd bounds farther away. The pack had been focused on this caribou from the start. It had been limping ever so slightly. The wolves know it is the easiest to catch.

The lead female wolf races in front of the caribou. Dashing back and forth, she blocks its path to the disappearing herd. She is the quickest wolf, but the males are stronger. They take down the trembling prey. After the kill, the lead male and female eat first.

The remaining members of a pack feed after the alpha male and female.

The other adults and the pups wait their turn. The young wolves had tagged along to observe the hunt. They will show what they have learned when they grow bigger.

Almost Lost

For centuries people have feared wolves. When food is scarce, these predators sometimes hunt farmers' livestock. The animals have become a symbol for evil. Stories such as "Little Red Riding Hood" and *Peter and the Wolf* reflect these fears.

During the last two centuries, thousands of wolves have disappeared from the lower 48 states.

The Alexander Archipelago Wolf

The largest gray wolf population in the United States is found in Alaska. Between 7,000 and 11,200 members of the species live in this northernmost state. The Alexander Archipelago wolf is a subspecies of the gray wolf. A subspecies is a group of animals within a certain species that share certain features. The Alexander Archipelago wolf has darker fur than other gray wolves. This wolf subspecies has been decreasing in numbers due to hunting, trapping, and logging in Alaska's Tongass National Forest.

People often depict wolves as animals to be feared.

One of the biggest reasons is human activity. People have hunted and trapped gray wolves to near extinction. Humans have moved into the wolves' ranges. Many of these people become angry when wolves then trespass on claimed property.

Forced to Wander

Another threat to the gray wolf is the distance it must travel to reach its prey. When humans encroach on the wolves' habitats, they also displace other wildlife. Many of these animals make up the gray wolf's diet.

A gray wolf pack's territory may be as small as 50 square miles (130 sq km). If food is scarce, its territory can span a much wider area. Some packs must cover more than 50 miles (80 km) to locate prey. At one time wolves could travel this distance without ever seeing a person. Today wolves must often cross roads or private land as they hunt. They are more likely to stumble upon an angry property owner.

Loss of Protection

In 2011 the US Congress voted to remove some gray wolves from the Endangered Species List. These wolves lived across much of the Northern Rockies. Soon it was legal to hunt them in the fall and winter. States limited the number of wolves that could be hunted. The US District Court for the District of

Wolf packs have large territories. They might travel more than 50 miles (80 km) to find food.

Columbia reversed the decision in 2014. Wolves in the western Great Lakes region were protected again. But damage had been done to the wolf population.

More than 550 gray wolves were killed in 2013 in Idaho, Montana, and Wyoming. These were just three of eight states in which Congress had lifted the hunting bans. US Fish and Wildlife Service agents killed an additional 216 wolves the same year because they had attacked livestock.

Gray wolves are slowly recovering. Many conservationists still fear for the species's long-term survival. They are working to keep the population safe. Because of these efforts, the gray wolf's future is bright.

Easy Prey

When it became legal to hunt wolves again, people worried that killing too many adult wolves could cause another problem for livestock. Adult wolves play important roles in their packs. One vital role is helping to raise the younger wolves. When an adult is killed, it may leave behind pups. These pups learn to hunt from their elders. Without instruction, younger wolves are more likely to go after easier prey, such as farm animals.

Brian Hare and Vanessa Woods have spent years studying the connection between wolves and domesticated dogs. In *The Genius of Dogs*, the authors explain that people have long been a negative force in the wolf's struggle to survive:

> *Occasionally, there is a story of children who were adopted and raised by wolves with a happy ending, like Romulus and Remus, who went on to found Rome, or Mowgli in Rudyard Kipling's* Jungle Book. *But for the most part, no other animal has been portrayed so ubiquitously as the Bad Guy throughout history. . . .*
>
> *The revilement of wolves was not limited to myths and fables. Almost every human culture in the world that has come into contact with wolves has persecuted them at one time or another, and these persecutions have often led to their local annihilation.*

Source: Brian Hare and Vanessa Woods. The Genius of Dogs: How Dogs Are Smarter than You Think. *New York: Dutton, 2013. Print. 17–18.*

What's the Big Idea?

Read Hare and Woods's words carefully. Have you noticed examples of wolves as villainous characters in modern books and films? How do you think these stories affect people's views of real-life animals? How could people's poor opinions of wolves be changed?

CHAPTER TWO

A POWERFUL PREDATOR

Gray wolves were named for the color of their coats. This color may be any shade of gray. Not all members of this species are gray, though. Some are black, while others are white. Most are a combination of these colors. Although they look like large dogs, gray wolves are wild animals.

Male wolves can weigh 85 to 145 pounds (40–65 kg). Females are a bit smaller at 70 to

Gray wolves' coats come in a variety of shades of gray.

The Survival of Future Generations

There is a difference between surviving and thriving. An adult gray wolf can survive as long as it eats an average of 2.5 pounds (1.1 kg) of food each day. But this amount of food is not enough to allow wolves to reproduce. Females need to eat approximately 5 pounds (2.3 kg) of food a day to give birth to healthy pups. Pups must also eat enough food to live into adulthood. Without new generations, the species could soon become endangered again.

110 pounds (30–50 kg). Both reach their adult sizes at approximately one year old.

Gray wolves are powerful predators. Their keen senses of hearing and smell help them locate prey. Wolves hunt large hoofed animals, such as deer, elk, and moose. They also eat birds, fish, and small game, such as beavers and rabbits. When food is scarce, they will even eat animals that have died from other causes. Once wolves pick up on the scent of an animal, they move closer to it. Then they use their speed and agility to catch and kill it. A gray wolf can

Wolves often use body language to communicate.

eat 20 pounds (9 kg) of meat after a kill. It often goes several days without eating after a large meal.

Wolves are social animals. Packs of seven to eight wolves usually hunt together. A pack may travel 12 miles (20 km) in a single day. They are led by an alpha male and an alpha female. Wolves howl to communicate with the other members of their pack. A wolf howl is as unique as a human fingerprint. Scientists can identify a wolf by listening to this

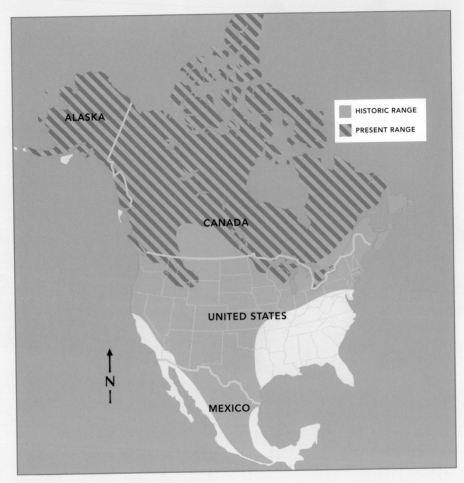

HISTORIC RANGE

PRESENT RANGE

ALASKA

CANADA

UNITED STATES

N

MEXICO

Past and Present Range

Look at the range map of the different locations where gray wolves have lived. What do you notice about the change in the wolf's range? How does this help you understand the gray wolf's situation today?

sound. Wolves can also identify their pack members by their howls. They also whine, bark, and growl to one another.

Gray Wolves and Their Environment

Gray wolves live in Canada, Alaska, and parts of the lower 48 states. A few live in the Pacific Northwest. Greater numbers reside in the Great Lakes region and the northern Rocky Mountains. Wyoming's Yellowstone National Park is also home to a large gray wolf population.

Gray wolves can survive in a variety of habitats. Those in Alaska live in tundra, as well as boreal and temperate rainforests. Most wolves in the lower 48 states live in

Changing Numbers

The number of wolves in an area can rise or fall greatly within short periods of time. A population can double in two to three years under the right conditions. Wolves reproduce quickly. If prey is plentiful, more pups will survive into adulthood. Laws that ban hunting wolves also play a big role. Still, populations can decline quickly if people kill too many wolves in a short period of time. For these reasons, many people feel it is important not to remove hunting bans too soon. Wildlife management can help balance wolf numbers.

Wolves keep Yellowstone's elk from overpopulating. Having fewer elk helps aspen trees grow.

forests and mountains. But they will go where they must to find food.

The gray wolf has a huge effect on other wildlife. It even affects plants in its area. Wolves hunt deer. Without wolves, deer can overpopulate and eat too many plants. They will eat some plants faster than the plants can grow. Some plants may come close to extinction. Then deer have trouble finding food. They may starve. Wolves help maintain the balance of many living things.

While wolves mostly hunt wild animals, they also sometimes hunt livestock. A gray wolf can smell animals such as sheep from miles away. They do not understand the difference between wild prey animals and livestock.

Wolves must eat in order to survive. But when the gray wolf threatens livestock, it threatens its own survival. Most farmers do not want to kill wolves. But they also cannot allow wolves to kill their animals. This dilemma threatens the gray wolf population.

FURTHER EVIDENCE

Chapter Two contains information about the areas in which gray wolves live. What do you think is the main point of the chapter? What evidence was given to support that point? Visit the website below to learn more about threats to the gray wolf. Choose a quote from the website that relates to this chapter. Does this quote support the author's main point? Does it make a new point? Write a few sentences explaining how the quote you found relates to this chapter.

Delisting the Gray Wolf in Oregon
mycorelibrary.com/gray-wolf

CHAPTER THREE

ONGOING THREATS

The biggest threat to the gray wolf's survival is humans. People have killed wolves for centuries. In the past, gray wolves were also hunted and trapped for their fur. Over time the species began to suffer as a whole. Too many wolves were killed. Hunting wolves was outlawed in most states while wolves were on the Endangered Species List from 1978 to 2009. Wolves in Alaska have never

People have long hunted wolves for their fur.

Sometimes wolves kill livestock such as these sheep in Montana. Farmers or wildlife agents may then kill the wolves.

been listed as endangered. Their numbers have been healthy. Today hunting is legal in some other states, such as Idaho.

Today some people kill wolves whether it is legal or not. Others are simply trying to protect their farm animals. When humans move into wolves' territory, prey becomes hard to find. Wolves must move to locate food. Sometimes their hunger leads them to farms.

Wolves that attack farm animals become problems for farmers. The number of cattle killed by wolves in the United States jumped from 4,400 to 8,100 between 2005 and 2010. The farmers rely on these animals for their livelihoods. They must protect their flocks. Often they will kill wolves that come onto their land.

The Hunting Controversy

Wolf hunting and trapping are controversial topics. In 2009 Idaho and Montana began issuing wolf-hunting permits.

Problems at the State Level

Conservation groups worry that state laws will hurt gray wolves. As national protections are removed, each state must manage its own wolf population. When wolves attack livestock, many states respond by allowing hunts. But some people think that hunting wolves is a bad idea. The species's numbers have improved greatly, but they are far from high. A species becomes vulnerable to extinction when there are fewer than 10,000 living adult members. There may be as few as 13,205 gray wolves left in the United States. Many people argue that hunting could quickly set back gray wolf recovery.

Some people were happy with this move. But others protested it. They worried that there were not enough wolves for the population to survive being hunted. They feared that wolves would become endangered again.

Some who favor hunting and trapping insist that conservationists will never see these activities as a reasonable option. Others say that legal kills can in fact increase livestock attacks. One study showed that in the year after a farmer killed a wolf, attacks on that farm's animals rose. The researchers suspect this might be due to the effects killings have on packs. When a lead wolf is killed, packs often break up. Young wolves are then forced to hunt alone and are more likely to raid farms.

Still, farmers need a way to protect their animals. Some people suggest farmers use firecrackers to scare away wolves. Farmers can use strong or electric fencing to keep the animals off private property. Red or orange flags strung around the fence can also deter

Oregon will allow wolf kills only if farmers have first tried nonlethal methods.

How Dogs Can Help

Livestock guardian dogs have long protected farm animals from wolves and other large predators. Today they help wolf conservation. Farmers can prevent wolf attacks by using these working dogs. Common breeds in North America include the akbash dog, Anatolian shepherd, and Great Pyrenees. The dogs live with the livestock. When wolves howl, these bold dogs bark or howl back. Neither animal wants a fight. The dogs often discourage the wolves before any animals get hurt.

wolves. Livestock guardian dogs that live with the animals often discourage wolves from attacking. Many farmers use these methods of preventing attacks. However, these techniques do not work all the time.

Encroachment

Another threat to gray wolves is human encroachment. Wolves require a great deal of space with specific conditions. They need a den, a water source, and plenty of prey. When people move into wolves' territories, they break up this space. The animals often end up with only part of what they need. To survive,

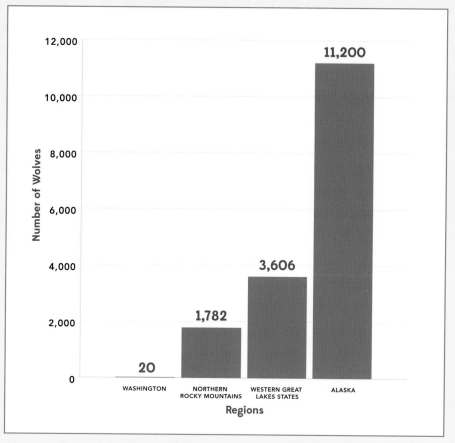

Wolves by the Numbers
This graph shows the highest estimate of wolves living in different areas of the United States in the mid-2010s. After reading about the gray wolf, where did you think the largest populations lived? What do you think these numbers looked like ten years ago?

they must then choose between moving to another region and staying where people live.

Risk comes with either choice. If the wolves cannot find food or water in a new range, they

As humans move into wolf habitats, they create new dangers, such as roads.

can die. But living too close to humans can be even more dangerous. Although wolves in North America rarely attack humans, most people fear them. This fear puts the wolves' lives at risk.

Many wolves have been able to find new habitats and thrive in them. Animals living in protected areas, such as national parks, are safe from human harm. But people are still developing land elsewhere. This further shrinks wolves' ranges and continues the threats posed by encroachment.

EXPLORE ONLINE

The focus of Chapter Three was on threats that gray wolves are still facing. The website below focuses on the same topic. As you know, every source is different. How is the information in the website different from the information in this chapter? What information is the same? What information did you learn from the website?

How New Laws Might Hurt Gray Wolves
mycorelibrary.com/gray-wolf

CHAPTER FOUR

THE FUTURE OF THE GRAY WOLF

The gray wolf species has come a long way in recent decades. The biggest population increases came under the federal Endangered Species Act (ESA). The ESA led to the creation of the Endangered Species List. The gray wolf was placed on that list in 1978. Killing or harming wolves became illegal in many areas. The ESA created a recovery plan

Alaska has the most wolves in the United States.

for gray wolves. It set aside time, energy, and money for conservation work.

Wolf populations have increased greatly since then. Researchers began documenting wolf populations in 1979 to track their status. In the late 1970s, Minnesota had between 1,000 and 1,200 wolves. By the late 1980s, that number had increased to nearly 1,750 wolves. Further studies showed that the species grew well into the 1990s. In the 1990s, conservation groups reintroduced wolves to Yellowstone National Park. Those wolves spread to Idaho and Montana. The wolves' range was expanding. The species was well on its way to recovery.

But the wolves' status has been controversial. Some people worry that problems will occur if wolf populations rise too quickly. Others think the species will suffer if protections are removed. So wolves have repeatedly been removed and relisted in different regions. In 2007 wolves in the western Great Lakes

People protested Minnesota wolf hunts in 2012.

and northern Rocky Mountains lost their endangered status. In April 2009, all wolves except those in Wyoming were taken off the list. Later that year, wolves in the western Great Lakes returned to the list. Wolf hunting was also banned in Idaho and Montana. The controversies remain today.

Everyday Citizens Make a Difference

The US House of Representatives introduced more than 80 proposals to limit the ESA in 2015 alone. One proposal would remove the gray wolf from the list. It was added to a large government spending bill. The bill was very long. Many representatives did not have time to read it. But thousands of Americans spoke out against the proposals. They helped ensure that the proposals were excluded from the final bill. They made a difference for the gray wolf by raising their voices.

Keeping Their Eyes on the Wolves

There is still hope for the species. Today there may be more than 16,705 wolves in the United States. Up to 11,200 of those live in Alaska. Researchers continue to study gray wolf populations around the country. Wolves are thriving in many places. But researchers know that they must keep their eyes on the numbers. State wolf management plans track these numbers. They set limits on how many wolves can be hunted or trapped. They also help farmers with wolf management.

Researchers use radio collars to track wolves.

Some organizations help ensure that laws protecting wolves are effective. Not everyone abides by the laws that protect wolves. When people kill wolves illegally, the Humane Society of the United States offers rewards for information that helps police identify and arrest culprits.

Dangerous Changes

Conservation groups, such as Defenders of Wildlife, keep a close eye on changing laws. Both state and federal legislation can reverse the progress the gray wolf has made. When a representative suggests a bill that threatens wolves' survival, these groups tell the public. They encourage people to contact their legislators and express their thoughts about the measure. Conservation groups also contact government officials directly to discuss the problem. The groups try to offer solutions that work for everyone. Other times these groups ask the courts for help to protect a species.

How Farmers Can Help Save Wolves

Farmers can help the gray wolf population by preventing livestock attacks. Keeping their animals in good health can make a difference. Wolves seek out the weakest and easiest prey. Wolves are less likely to attack healthy livestock. Farmers can also keep several livestock guardian dogs with herds. These guard dogs often deter wolves. Farmers can keep newborn calves or sheep in safer spots closer to the

Livestock guardian dogs live with and protect farm animals.

barns. Like sick animals, young animals often make easy targets for wolves.

The Gray Wolves of Tomorrow

The gray wolf's long-term survival depends heavily on education and scientifically based management. When people learn more about gray wolves, they can help this species thrive. Farmers can learn how to prevent wolf attacks. Other people can help by campaigning to maintain gray wolf populations. But reliable information is necessary. Conservation groups and groups that favor wolf hunting can be biased. The best way to judge how gray wolves are doing is by comparing what each group says and by reading scientific studies.

One of the biggest risks that the gray wolf faces is changes to federal laws. Some members of Congress have suggested delisting wolves altogether. This would leave the wolves with no protection. Some people think that changing the wolf's status to threatened would be better. This would allow farmers to kill wolves when necessary but protect the species from being hunted. In the end, it is up to people to ensure the future of gray wolves is secure.

Adrian Wydeven is the lead wolf biologist for the Wisconsin Department of Natural Resources. He explains how keeping the gray wolf on the Endangered Species List could hurt the animals:

> I believe continued listing of wolves as endangered will further erode attitudes toward wolves within the Great Lakes region. Without delisting, states would have little ability to reduce abundance of wolves. . . . Landowners will become frustrated in their inability to protect pets and livestock on their property, and difficulty in obtaining federal trapping of problem wolves. Rates of illegal kill will likely increase on wolves. Oppositions to wolves in rural areas will likely continue to grow. . . . Continued wolf listing would frustrate efforts by the states to manage the wolves and create animosity toward wolves throughout rural areas. Management of wolves would likely become more chaotic and unstable in the region.
>
> Source: Melissa Higgs. "Interview with Adrian Wydeven." Springer. Springer Science+Business Media, n.d. Web. Accessed May 3, 2016.

Back It Up

Take a close look at Wydeven's words. What is his main idea? What evidence is used to support his point? Write a few sentences showing how Wydeven uses two or three pieces of evidence to support his main point.

SPECIES OVERVIEW

Common Name

- Gray wolf

Scientific Name

- *Canis lupus*

Average Size

- 26 to 32 inches (66–81 cm) tall at the shoulder;
  4.5 to 6 feet (1.4–1.8 meters) long from nose to tail
- 85 to 145 pounds (40–65 kg) for adult males;
  70 to 110 pounds (30–50 kg) for adult females (northern
  wolves are larger than those in the lower 48 states)

Color

- Any shade of gray, black, or white—most gray wolves are
  a combination of these colors

Diet

- Hoofed animals such as boar, deer, and elk; smaller
  animals such as beavers, rabbits, birds, fish, and reptiles.
  When food is scarce, wolves may also attack livestock.

Average Life Span

- Up to 13 years in the wild; 15 years or more in captivity

Habitat

- North American forests, grasslands, mountains, woodlands, and tundra

Threats

- Conflicts with farmers, landscape modification, encroachment, uncontrolled hunting and trapping
- Endangered status: endangered

STOP AND THINK

Surprise Me

Chapter One shared some interesting information about the gray wolf species. After reading this book, what two or three facts from the chapter did you find most surprising? Why did you find each fact surprising?

Say What?

Learning about species that have faced endangerment can mean learning a lot of new vocabulary. Find five words in this book that you had never seen or heard before. Use a dictionary to find out what they mean. Then write the meanings in your own words and use each word in a new sentence.

Tell the Tale

Chapter Three discusses the threat of encroachment to the gray wolf population. Write 200 words from the point of view of a wolf that was forced to leave its habitat due to encroachment. Make sure to set the scene, develop a sequence of events, and include a conclusion.

You Are There

This book discusses how gray wolves hunt. Imagine you are observing a hunt. What might you notice about the gray wolves you see? What do you notice about the prey? What does the landscape look like? Be sure to add plenty of detail to your notes.

GLOSSARY

animosity
great resentment or dislike

annihilation
complete destruction

biased
having unfair feelings or
opinions that one thing is
better than another

conservation
preserving and protecting
something

encroach
to move onto another's
property little by little

overpopulate
to increase in numbers to the
point of causing problems

predator
an animal that hunts and eats
other animals

range
an area where an animal lives

species
a group of animals or plants
that share basic traits

subspecies
a group of animals within a
species that share basic traits
different from the rest of the
species

territory
an area where animals live
and find food

ubiquitous
widespread or universally
accepted

LEARN MORE

Books

Gagne, Tammy. *Tundra Ecosystems.* Minneapolis: Abdo Publishing, 2016.

Marsh, Laura. *Wolves.* Washington, DC: National Geographic, 2012.

Somervill, Barbara A. *Gray Wolf.* Ann Arbor, MI: Cherry Lake, 2008.

Websites

To learn more about Back from Near Extinction, visit **booklinks.abdopublishing.com**. These links are routinely monitored and updated to provide the most current information available.

Visit **mycorelibrary.com** for free additional tools for teachers and students.

INDEX

ABOUT THE AUTHOR

Tammy Gagne has written more than 150 books for adults and children. She resides in northern New England with her husband and son. One of her favorite pastimes is visiting schools to talk to kids about the writing process.